THE WINNER'S FAITH

For whatsoever is born of God overcometh the world: and this is the victory that overcometh the world, even our faith.
1 John 5:4

by

Franklin N. Abazie

The Winner's Faith
COPYRIGHT@ 2017 BY Franklin N Abazie
ISBN: 978-1-945133-37-4

All right reserved. This book or any portion thereof may not be reproduced or used in any manner whatsoever without the express written permission of the publisher, except for the use of brief quotations in a book review. All Bible quotes are from King James Version and others as noted.

Published by: F N ABAZIE PUBLISHING HOUSE- aka, Empowerment Bookstore.

That I may publish with the voice of thanksgiving and tell of all thy wondrous works.
Psalms 26:7

To order additional copies, wholesales
or booking:
Call the Church office (973-372-7518),
or Empowerment Bookstore Hotline (973-393-8518)

Worship address:
343 Sanford Avenue Newark New Jersey 07106
Administrative Head Office address:
33 Schley Street Newark New Jersey 07112
Email:pastorfranknto@yahoo.com
Website www.fnabaziehealingministries.org
Publishing House: www.fnabaziepublishinghouse.org

This book is a production of F N Abazie Publishing House.
A publication Arms of Miracle of God Ministries 2017.
First Edition

CONTENTS

THE MANDATE OF THE COMMISSION .. iv

ARMS OF THE COMMISSION v

INTRODUCTION vi

1 THE MENTALITY OF A WINNER 1

2 OVERCOMING CHALLENGES 21

3 PRAYER OF SALVATION 62

4 ABOUT THE AUTHOR 73

THE MANDATE OF THE COMMISSION

"The moment is due to impact your world through the revival of the healing & miracle ministry of Jesus Christ of Nazareth.

I am sending you to restore health unto thee and I will heal thee of thy wounds. Said the Lord of Host."

ARMS OF THE COMMISSION

1) F N Abazie Ministries-Miracle of God Ministries (Miracle Chapel Intl)

2) F N Abazie TV Ministries: Global Television Ministry Outreach.

3) F N Abazie Radio Ministries: Radio Broadcasting Outreach.

4) F N Abazie Publishing House: Book Publication.

5) F N Abazie Bible School: also called Word of Healing Bible School (W.O.H.B.S)

6) F N Abazie Evangelistic Ass: Miracle of God Ministries: Global Crusade

7) Empowerment Bookstore: Book distribution.

8) F N Abazie Helping Hands: Meeting the help of the needy world wide

9) F N Abazie Disaster Recovery Mission: Global Disaster Recovery.

10) F N Abazie Prison Ministry: Prison Ministry for all convicts "Second chance."

Some of our ministry arms are waiting the appointed time to commence.

INTRODUCTION

"For whatsoever is born of God overcometh the world: and this is the victory that overcometh the world, even our faith."
1 John 5:4

Among my deep findings and discovery in scriptures is the reward and mentality of winners, from the bible. Although everyone wants to win in life, unless we are in command of the winning secrets in life, we will forever struggle to succeed and win in any area of life.

Life is a race and we all must run to win the prize. *" Know ye not that they which run in a race run all, but one receiveth the prize? So run, that ye may obtain."* (1 Cor 9:24) Zig Ziglar once said "You were born to win, but to be a winner, you must plan to win, prepare to win, and expect to win." Zig Ziglar."

If you ask even a dummy he/she want to win in life. Nobody wants to be associated with failure in life. *"And he that overcometh, and keepeth my works unto the end, to him will I give power over the nations:"* (Rev 2:29).

In this small book and as revealed by the Holy Spirit, we have tried to enlighten every reader that as long as we develop faith to fight to the end we will emerge winners in our desired area in life.

" He that overcometh, the same shall be clothed in white raiment..."
Rev 3:5

For the most part, winning comes with a sacrifice, for anyone to win, we must be disciplined, dedicated, devoted, and make plenty of personal sacrifice. *"We must pay the price if we must win the prize."*

For us to win in life we must trust God, have faith in God and faith in our individual ability to win in any area of our desire. I am trusting God that as you read this book, the winner in you must emerge and with speed. Read and be blessed.

For whatsoever is born of God overcometh the world: and this is the victory that overcometh the world, even our faith.

Who is he that overcometh the world, but he that believeth that Jesus is the Son of God
1 John 5:4-5

HIS DESTINY WAS THE
CROSS....

HIS PURPOSE WAS
LOVE.....

HIS REASON WAS
YOU....

WINNING SECRET

Among the secret to win in life is the secret of dedication, devotion, determination, hard work, patience, endurance wisdom, personal sacrifice, and understanding. In my opinion Christianity means taking responsibility of our life. We must recognize our strength and weakness before we make certain decisions in life. You are certain to get the worst of the bargain when you exchange ideas with the wrong person. In this race of life, always make friends with those who can inspire you, those you can learn from. The bible says He that walketh with wise men shall be wise: but a companion of fools shall be destroyed

Try to always be able to differentiate those God planted into your life for a season and for a long term. Information and continual learning is the key to succeed in life. Always chose your friends wisely, for evil companion corrupt good manners. Remember *"he that walk with the wise shall be wise."*

In the time of prosperity we recognize our friends. *"Wealth maketh many friends."* (Proverb 19:4) But in the time of adversity our friends know us, *"and there is a friend that sticketh closer than a brother."* (Proverb 18:24)

Always recognize those who make you a special person in their lives. Never make people significant in your life when you are only an option to them. The less you associate with some people the more your life will improve. Remember Abraham did not become rich until he separated from lot his nephew.

"And the Lord said unto Abram, after that Lot was separated from him, Lift up now thine eyes, and look from the place where thou art northward, and southward, and eastward, and westward: For all the land which thou seest, to thee will I give it, and to thy seed for ever."
Genesis 13:14-15

Anytime time you allow mediocrity in others, it increases your mediocrity. An important attribute in successful people is their impatience with failure, negative thinking, and mediocrity. As we grow in life, our association will eventually change over time.

Eventually, you will disconnect from those that failed to improve their lives and you will connect and make friends with other successful people going up higher in the race of life. Never receive counsel from unproductive negative thinking people, never discus your trial and challenges with those incapable of contributing to the solution or solving your problems. Always look for the best in people around you. Develop a forgiving heart, a thankful countenance, and praiseful spirit.

Always remember this, if you are going to achieve excellence in big things, you must develop the habit in little matters. Collin Powell once said and I quote *"A dream doesn't become a reality through magic, it takes sweat, determination, and hard work."* There is no secret to success, it is the result of preparation, hard work, and learning from failure. Excellence is not an exception, it is a prevailing attitude.

WINNERS ATTITUDE

----- *Always carry a mental picture of your actual future.*

If you always believe what you see, touch, and feel you will end up a failure in life. As long as you believe in God , we can change any bad habit into a good one.

-----*Always be positive in life.*

Always see the good and a way out of any impossible situation in life. If He divided the red sea into two, how much more shall he not freely give you your heart desires in life? *"He that spared not his own Son, but delivered him up for us all, how shall he not with him also freely give us all things?"*

-----*Always believe that every day is a good day for you.*

Always expect the best out of each and every day of your life. Always see every day you wake up as a day of blessing and favor in your life. There is no bad day in life. Never say this is a bad day for me.

----- *Always be optimistic in life regardless of prevailing outcome.*

Unless we see opportunities out of every challenge in life, we shall never overcome any obstacle in life. Always see something good out of the most obscure and unpredictable situation. It is proven, as long as we are expecting something good. Somethings will eventually happen for us in life.

Think like a winner.

1) Always remember that your present situation is not your final destination. The best is yet to come.

2) Sometimes the bad things that happens in our lives put us directly on the path of the best things that will ever happen to us.

3) If you don't like where you are, move. You are not a tree.

4) You can't start the next chapter if you keep reading the last.

5) If it doesn't open, it's not your door. Watch it!

6) Sometimes you need to stop outside, get some air, and remind yourself of who you are and where you want to be.

7) Sometimes you need to talk to a three year old, just so you can understand life again.

8) Listen & silent are spelled with the same letters. Think about it.

9) Sometimes, you have to stop thinking so much and just go where your heart takes you.

10) You don't have to have it all figured out to move forward.

11) Never stop believing because miracles happen every day.

MEEKNESS

It is written *"The meek will he guide in judgment: and the meek will he teach his way."* (Psalms 25:9)

Unless we are humbled and willing to learn in life we will never win. God lifts us up in life, only when we are humbled in the spirit. It is written *"...he bringeth down to the grave, and bringeth up. The Lord maketh poor, and maketh rich: he bringeth low, and lifteth up. He raiseth up the poor out of the dust, and lifteth up the beggar from the dunghill, to set them among princes, and to make them inherit the throne of glory:.."*
(1 Samuel 2:6-8)

Meekness is the flat form for victory and success in life. Our life will never change or go up as long as we remain proud, arrogant and with an unteachable spirit. I prophesy to you, embrace meekness and watch God decorate your life in the mighty name of Jesus.

WILLINGNESS TO TRAIN

It is proven we only master our trade by training. I was never a good speaker until I began learning, reading, and listening to more sermons on a daily bases. Unless we continue to train up ourselves, we will never develop ourselves to the level of a winner in any area of life (finances, marriage, career, academics. (e.t.c).

Training is the best secret of winning in life. In my opinion training grants confidence and assurance. Every time we train very well in any area of life we master our trade. I encourage you today to go back into training our mind and our body to face the challenges that are opposing our life in the mighty Name of Jesus.

WILLINGNESS TO LEARN FROM MISTAKES AND PAST FAILURES...

Unless we are humbled to learn from our mistakes and past failures, we will never win in life. God is a God of a second chance. He gives us the opportunity to improve our lives. We must embrace humility, and learn from our mistakes, and past failures, take correction, and instruction as needed from our mentors and masters in life.

"Till I come, give attendance to reading, to exhortation, to doctrine."
1 Timothy 4:13

DEVELOP A POSITIVE ATTITUDE TOWARDS EVERY CHALLENGE IN LIFE

The Lord said to me January 6th 2017 while driving to New York City from New Jersey and reflecting on some prevailing financial challenges and my law school degree and career change, that *"Developing a positive attitude towards every challenge in life is the key to success and victorious living."* ---Franklin N Abazie

In my opinion a positive attitude is the secret key to confront challenges and opposition in life. Every time we exhibit a positive attitude out of faith in God, we overcome and dominate every opposition, trials, and tribulation in life. Instead of fear and intimidation from threats, almost all winners in life, see every threats as opportunity in life. Positive attitude makes us calm in the midst of great calamities and destruction in life. I encourage you today, irrespective of your trials and your story, develop a positive attitude and watch God grant you unprecedented victorious in life.

The story about Caleb on the report on the exploration of the land will inspires us about positive attitude in life.

"They came back to Moses and Aaron and the whole Israelite community at Kadesh in the Desert of Paran. There they reported to them and to the whole assembly and showed them the fruit of the land. They gave Moses this account: "We went into the land to which you sent us, and it does flow with milk and honey! Here is its fruit. But the people who live there are powerful, and the cities are fortified and very large. We even saw descendants of Anak there. The Amalekites live in the Negev; the Hittites, Jebusites and Amorites live in the hill country; and the Canaanites live near the sea and along the Jordan. Then Caleb silenced the people before Moses and said, "We should go up and take possession of the land, for we can certainly do it."

Number 13:26-30 NIV

WHAT IS A POSITIVE ATTITUDE IN LIFE?

A positive attitude in life is our ability to be strong and encouraged in the midst of calamities. It is our ability to be bold and confident in the midst of the obstacles and challenges of life. Unless we gather courage to confront our fears and doubts in life, we will never emerge winners in life. In my own opinion, the fact that we are saved from our sins, baptized, and speak in tongue, does not exempt us from facing difficult oppositions, challenges, hardship, hindrances, and the obstacles of life.

"These things I have spoken unto you, that in me ye might have peace. In the world ye shall have tribulation: but be of good cheer; I have overcome the world".
John 16:33

It is written *"But my servant Caleb, because he had another spirit with him, and hath followed me fully, him will I bring into the land where into he went; and his seed shall possess it."* (Number 14:24)

We must therefore develop faith and establish dominion in our lives to confront and overcome any prevailing challenge that oppose us in life.

CHAPTER 1
THE MENTALITY OF A WINNER

"For whatsoever is born of God overcometh the world: and this is the victory that overcometh the world, even our faith."
1 John 5:4

Quite frankly, all winners in life think alike. Their eyes are focused on the prize. They pay great attention to the prize because of the reward attached to it. If I'm permitted to put it this way, *"All winners in life aspire to acquire the desires they admire in life."* But unless we define what it means to win, it will be difficult to talk about the mentality of a winner without defining the word *"winner, or what it means to win."*

The American College dictionary defined winning as to achieve victory or finish first in a competition, to achieve success in an effort or a venture, to receive a prize or reward for performance. To achieve or attain by effort, to obtain or earn livelihood. In the context of this text, we are talking of the faith of every winner. All winners in life, are passionate serious like-minded people like me and you, they develop a strong passion and a positive attitude towards winning in life. They are faithful men/women who focus and put all their positive energy in to one thing.

"Men of impact are men of influence, and men of influence are winner in life, for they rule the world"- (Franklin N Abazie 2017)

Although every winner in life think alike, the mentality of every winner is focused on success and the rewards attached to it in life. *"Wealth maketh many friends; but the poor is separated from his neighbour."*
Proverb 19:4

Life is a race, and therefore everyone running the race of life must be determined to make an impact and emerge with victory and success in life.

Successful men/women never consider failure as an option in life. The life of every successful men and women is driven by their passion to succeed in life. The goal of successful men/women is to win in whatever area of their interest and become successful in their area of interest in life. We as believers must embrace the same mentality.

The art of winning (a game, a deal, a match, a prize or even winning gift items or money) is very important to Jesus Christ. It is written *"Let them shout for joy, and be glad, that favour my righteous cause: yea, let them say continually, Let the Lord be magnified, which hath pleasure in the prosperity of his servant."* (Psalms 35:27)

"Him that overcometh will I make a pillar in the temple of my God, and he shall go no more out: and I will write upon him the name of my God, and the name of the city of my God, which is new Jerusalem, which cometh down out of heaven from my God: and I will write upon him my new name."
Rev 3:12

According to scriptures we are created to be winners in every area of our life not just spiritually but financially, professionally, in our relationships and in every other area of life. It is written *"And God blessed them, and God said unto them, Be fruitful, and multiply, and replenish the earth, and subdue it: and have dominion over the fish of the sea, and over the fowl of the air, and over every living thing that moveth upon the earth."* (Genesis 1:28)

WHAT IS THE FAITH OF A WINNER?

Winning means everything to the believer. It's the only thing that determines our faith in God. However, some believers lose at one point in their life or the other. To win means to succeed. Whenever we become successful in life we attract so many friends.

"Wealth maketh many friends; but the poor is separated from his neighbour."
Proverb 19:4

To me, the faith of the winner is determination to succeed and win the prize. It is the dedication to focus to the end. The faith of the winner literally means devotion and dedication to a cause and the drive and motivation to succeed regardless of the prevailing challenges in life.

Success in life is not a magic, we must embrace small beginning, learn from our weakness and failure, be driven with a purpose, and be determined with stamina to endure to the end. Collin Powell once said *"There are no secrets to success. It is the result of preparation, hard work, and learning from failure."* He said *"A dream doesn't become reality through magic, it takes sweat, determination, and hard work."* Success, therefore is the result of preparation, perfection, hard work, and learning from failure, loyalty, and persistence in life.

WHAT ARE WE SAYING?

For anyone to succeed in life, we must be willing, determined and persistent and driven to succeed in life. Every successful business man/woman or any accomplished sports hero who have been through life ups and down, and still succeeds is a winner in life. We all want to win but we do not want to face the reality of life challenges and obstacles.

The truth is every winners bounces back, as long as we have faith in God and a winning mentality inside of our heart. Winners are faithful people who believe they will win in any prevailing competition. Every winner and champion in life, is always optimistic in life, they are positive men and women who put in all their energy into their desire goal in life. These are men/women of discipline, determination, dedication, and sacrifice. These set of people look at the goal and not at the race at hand. These set of people focus on the result- the end product.

"To him that overcometh will I grant to sit with me in my throne, even as I also overcame, and am set down with my Father in his throne."
Rev 3:21

"However difficult life may seem, there is always something you can do and succeed at"----- Stephen Hawking

TRAITS OF WINNING IN LIFE
--- *Remain inspired despite all odds*---

"Then he said unto them, Go your way, eat the fat, and drink the sweet, and send portions unto them for whom nothing is prepared: for this day is holy unto our Lord: neither be ye sorry; for the joy of the Lord is your strength."
Nehemiah 8:10

If we must win in life we must embrace the positive attitude of joy and happiness. Good mood and positive feeling about winning inspires us to confront any prevailing challenges of life. Clearly everyone feels good about winning, while emotions sag at failure. The truth is that, our emotions affects our performance in life. Positive moods produce physical energy and the resilience to persist after setbacks. Most winners in life never quit. It is proven that losers in life will always find an excuse or who to blame and quit.

" Thou wilt shew me the path of life: in thy presence is fulness of joy; at thy right hand there are pleasures for evermore."
Psalm 16:11

I encourage you to embrace a winning spirit despite the adversaries we may encounter in life.

--The Love of God--

Unless we embrace the love of God in our heart, we will forever remain in despair and despondency. The love of God is the key to every winning life. King Solomon became the wealthiest in his time, not because of his wisdom and understanding, but because he loved the Lord with all his heart. If we must win in all our life challenges we must embrace the love of God with passion *"And Solomon loved the Lord, walking in the statutes of David his father: only he sacrificed and burnt incense in high places."* (1 King 3:3)

-- Learning from past failures and mistakes--

Collin Powell once said *"There are no secrets to success: don't waste time looking for them. Success is the result of perfection, hard work, learning from failure, loyalty to those for whom you work, and persistence. Most losers in life get defensive, avoids negative and constructive feedbacks, and looks for who to blame. The idea of making excuses in life are very detrimental to any great destiny."*

"And they all with one consent began to make excuse. The first said unto him, I have bought a piece of ground, and I must needs go and see it: I pray thee have me excused. And another said, I have bought five yoke of oxen, and I go to prove them: I pray thee have me excused. And another said, I have married a wife, and therefore I cannot come."
Luke 14:18-20

Every winner must be someone who deal and confronts every obstacle and prevailing challenges in life. Every winner in life are more likely to voluntarily discuss mistakes and accept negative feedback, and learn from their mistakes and failures in life.

"For a just man falleth seven times, and riseth up again: but the wicked shall fall into mischief."
Proverb 24:16

Winners are confident men and women in life who always sees the possibility of winning and succeeding despite the obstacles confronting them in life. Most winner embraces challenges as an opportunity for their rising in life. …………

….Remember the story of David and Goliath. (See 1 Samuel 17)

------*Focus on one thing*------

Unless we are sold out for one thing and one thing alone in life, we will forever misuse our time and misplace our priority in life. The key to every winning life is focus. It is proven that every time we put all our energy in one thing with a zeal of the Lord and a determined heart, we win easily.

" Brethren, I count not myself to have apprehended: but this one thing I do, forgetting those things which are behind, and reaching forth unto those things which are before, I press toward the mark for the prize of the high calling of God in Christ Jesus."
Phil 3:13-14

If we must win in any area of our life we must embrace paying attention unto one thing and one thing alone in life. Jesus made it clear to us.

"And Jesus said unto him, No man, having put his hand to the plough, and looking back, is fit for the kingdom of God."
Luke 9:62.

One of my greatest moment in life was responding to my wife question on how I was going to New York law school for a Juris Doctorate Degree in law, and at the same time, keep up with my independent contracting job and also pastor the ministry. Focus and attention to details of the pressing issue at hand is the key. In my opinion our ability to recognize our weakness and strength, threats and opportunities is the key to a winning life of victory.

--Right Foundation in God--

We are told *"If the foundations be destroyed, what can the righteous do?"* (Psalm 11:3) Our foundation must be right with God if we must win in life. Life is a warfare and not a fun fare. Daniel said *"... but the people that do know their God shall be strong, and do exploits."* (Daniel 11:32) Joseph commanded exploit because he knew his God. David commanded great victories against the philistine and the Amalekites because his foundation was right in God. We develop a right foundation in God if we must emerge winners in any area of interest in life.

--Develop personal relationship with the Holy Spirit--

Unless we develop fellowship and relationship with the person of the Holy Spirit we forever miss the prize of success in life. In my opinion knowing the person of the Holy Spirit is the key to all victorious living and winning in life. The Holy Spirit as the comforter will not leave us helpless in life.

"But the Comforter, which is the Holy Ghost, whom the Father will send in my name, he shall teach you all things, and bring all things to your remembrance, whatsoever I have said unto you."
John 14:26

--Self-determination--

We must be self-determined if we must win in life. Determination I believe is the key to success in life. Unless we are determined to succeed in life, we have indirectly planned to fail. We must be determined in life that we must make an impact in our life time. God restored the life of the prodigal son only when he was determined to return to his father. *"I will arise and go to my father, and will say unto him, Father, I have sinned against heaven, and before thee."* (Luke 15:18) Determination is the key to success. King Solomon built a house for God because he was determined. And Solomon determined to build an house for the name of the Lord, and an house for his kingdom. (2 Chronicle 2:2)

--Be dedicated to win life--

Winning and succeeding comes with great devotion, dedication, sacrifice, and personal efforts. Most of us love to win but hate to devote time to the tactics and strategy it take for us to succeed and win in life. If we must win in life we must take our life serious because our faith will determine our fate in life. Unless we take responsibility in life we will never taste success.

"Wealth gotten by vanity shall be diminished: but he that gathereth by labour shall increase."
Proverb 13:11

DEDICATION

Dedication means we must love our work. If you love what you do for a living, you will do it with excitement, delight and with joy. If you are dedicated at your work its only a question of time and you will breakthrough on every side

DISCIPLINE

As soldiers of Jesus Christ, we must be disciplined to succeed in life. *"Thou therefore endure hardness, as a good soldier of Jesus Christ."* (2 Timothy 2:3)

We must discipline our mind to align with our heart and hand. We must discipline our lifestyle to meet the demands of our career and future. We must be discipline to plan our life carefully to succeed. One great man said and I quote *"Discipline is the soul of an army. It makes small numbers formidable; procures success to the weak, and esteem to all."* - George Washington.

EXTRA PERSONAL EFFORTS

We must endeavor to make personal efforts in our life time. We must put in extra efforts for us to see supernatural results. Until we make personal sacrifice in the area of our calling we will not be able to fulfill our calling and destiny in life.

WHAT ARE WE SAYING?

No matter our present condition we must improve and strive to win. Remember the greatest room is the room for improvement. Never relent or rely on past accomplished glory. our God is never limited to give us more new things in life.

Remember......

"Now unto him that is able to do exceeding abundantly above all that we ask or think, according to the power that worketh in us."
Ephesians 3:20

WE MUST REPENT OF OUR SINS

"Create in me a clean heart, O God; and renew a right spirit within me. Cast me not away from thy presence; and take not thy holy spirit from me. Restore unto me the joy of thy salvation; and uphold me with thy free spirit."
Psalms 51:10-12

We must not allow sin to destroy our calling and destiny in life. We must therefore repent of any known sin in our lives before God can restore our destiny.

For sin shall not have dominion over you: for ye are not under the law, but under grace. (Romans 6:14)

Every time we yield to sin, we place ourselves in captivity. We must all strive to forsake sin and do away with every evil that dent our Christian dignity. Know ye not, that to whom ye yield yourselves servants to obey, his servants ye are to whom ye obey; whether of sin unto death, or of obedience unto righteousness? (Romans 6:16)

It is written, *"Be not overcome of evil, but overcome evil with good."* (Romans 12:21) We must all repent of any know sin that dents our Christian walk with the Lord Jesus Christ.

Apostle Paul had this to say....

"I find then a law, that, when I would do good, evil is present with me. For I delight in the law of God after the inward man: But I see another law in my members, warring against the law of my mind, and bringing me into captivity to the law of sin which is in my members. O wretched man that I am! who shall deliver me from the body of this death? I thank God through Jesus Christ our Lord. So then with the mind I myself serve the law of God; but with the flesh the law of sin."
Romans 7:21-25

If we consider our own life from the above scripture, it will be relevant for us to examine your own life. Think about it, evil is present every time we strive to do good.

"What shall we say then? Shall we continue in sin, that grace may abound? God forbid. How shall we, that are dead to sin, live any longer therein?"
Romans 6:1-2

"Examine yourselves, whether ye be in the faith; prove your own selves. Know ye not your own selves, how that Jesus Christ is in you, except ye be reprobates?"
2 Cor 13:5

Although most faith people live in denial about the work of the flesh, from my own scriptural understanding everyone operating within the scope of Galatians 5:20-21 is classified as a sinner.

How do I come out of sin?

Although we are all sinners, it takes a will power of the mind for us to repent and come out of sin. So many people and died because they could not let go the sin that easily best them go. Preacher who used to drug addicts have crashed and died because they went back into their addiction. A great man of God who repented because of alcohol in the family died of excessive alcohol abuse. We must make up our mind for good if we must come out of sin. We must confess, and forsake it in the mighty name of Jesus.

REPENT AND CONFESS THAT JESUS IS LORD. AMEN

The word says as many as received him, to them gave He power to become the sons of God. Even to them that believe on his name.

To qualify for divine visitation do the following sincerely

1) Acknowledge that you are a sinner and that He died for you.Rom3:23.

2) Repent of your sins. Acts 3:19, Luke13:5, 2Peter3:9

3) Believe in your heart that Jesus died for your sin.Romans10:10

4) Confess Jesus as the Lord over your life. Romans10:10, Acts 2:21

Now repeat this Prayer after me

Say Lord Jesus, I accept you today, as my Lord and my savior, forgive me of my sins wash me with your blood. Right now, I believe, I am sanctified, I am save, I am free, I am free from the Power of sin to serve the Lord Jesus. Thank you Lord for saving me. Amen.

Congratulations: YOU ARE NOW...

...A BORN AGAIN CHRISTIAN

AGAIN I SAY TO YOU - CONGRATULATIONS!

SUMMARY OF CHAPTER ONE

Say Lord Jesus give me the audacity to and the courage to develop the mentality of winner henceforth. I must win in any prevailing area of my life. (finances, marriage, career and academics.)

"Life is a warfare and not a fanfare"

We must therefore develop a meek and humble spirit for the winning spirit inside of us to emerge. The winners mentality means we must forever be progressive, better and improve our lives. Benjamin Franklin once said *"Without continual growth and progress, such words as improvement, achievement, and success have no meaning."*

"Sometimes we may ask God for success, and He gives us physical and mental stamina. We might plead for prosperity, and we receive enlarged perspective and increased patience, or we petition for growth and are blessed with the gift of grace. He may bestow upon us conviction and confidence as we strive to achieve worthy goals." - David A. Bednar

"Character cannot be developed in ease and quiet. Only through experience of trial and suffering can the soul be strengthened, ambition inspired, and success achieved." - Helen Keller

"Success consists of going from failure to failure without loss of enthusiasm." - Winston Churchill

"Always bear in mind that your own resolution to succeed is more important than any other." - Abraham Lincoln

Like Zig Ziglar once said we are born to win in life, but for us to win, we must plan to win, prepare to win and expect to win. I see you see you develop the mentality to succeed in your life time.

CHAPTER 2
OVERCOMING CHALLENGES

"These things I have spoken unto you, that in me ye might have peace. In the world ye shall have tribulation: but be of good cheer; I have overcome the world."
John 16:33

"There hath no temptation taken you but such as is common to man: but God is faithful, who will not suffer you to be tempted above that ye are able; but will with the temptation also make a way to escape, that ye may be able to bear it."
1 Cor 10:13

Our victory and strength in life is proportional to the challenges and the obstacles we overcome. Every prevailing obstacle or challenge is a set up for our next level in life. We must appreciate and embrace challenges in life for it tests our self-worth, develops our spiritual muscles, strengthens us and makes us overcomers in life. We must therefore as believers confront every challenge in life with faith in God believing that faithful is he who will help us overcome such trial or temptation in life. Whether we like it or not, adversity is part of our everyday life. Overcoming adversity among other challenges and obstacles of life is one of the primary test of our faith as Christians. As Havelock Ellis wrote, *"Pain and death are part of life. To reject them is to reject life itself."* Whether we bled the blood of Jesus or not trials and tribulations, present themselves to us throughout our whole existence just like Jesus reassured us in John sixteen verse thirty three.

The Christian faith teaches us how to confront and overcoming adversity in life. Overcoming challenges and obstacles in life builds us up, strengthens, us and puts us on the next level of our walk with God in life.

Every challenge we face in life is unique and peculiar to us per time in life. Herodotus, the Greek philosopher, said, *"Adversity has the effect of drawing out strength and qualities of a man that would have lain dormant in its absence."* It is erroneous to think money gives happiness like some folks think. But Nelson Mandela put it this way...

"Money won't create success, the freedom to make it will."- **Nelson Mandela**

Each person's success and happiness, both now and in the eternities, depend largely on his or her responses to the challenges and obstacles of life. Trials may come to us in life, as a consequence of a person's own pride and disobedience. Although these trials can be avoided through a good moral conscience and righteous lifestyle.

"There hath no temptation taken you but such as is common to man: but God is faithful, who will not suffer you to be tempted above that ye are able; but will with the temptation also make a way to escape, that ye may be able to bear it."
1 Cor 10:13

"For our light affliction, which is but for a moment, worketh for us a far more exceeding and eternal weight of glory."
2 Cor 4:17

Although there are some long term prevailing obstacles in life , most of our present challenges are seasonal in life. We must not magnify our trial, rather we must gather spiritual stamina to confront the hindrance or obstacle.

Hints to Overcome challenges in life

Acceptance:

Unless we embrace challenges as part of life, we will forever live in denial. Our mind is more productive when we accept seasonal obstacle and work our way out of it. Acknowledgment is the initial step towards a solution to the problem.

Develop mental strength:

Mental strength is the key to prevail against every obstacle in life. Unless we develop mental strength against the adversity or the enemy we will forever suffer defeat. It was mental strength that helped David to withstand Goliath of Gath in first Samuel chapter seventeen.

Information:

We are told by the Holy bible that my people perish for lack of knowledge. We must always be current and abreast with relevant information against any prevailing obstacle against our lives.

Remain inspired regardless of the odds:

Permit me to say this, for it takes inspiration to aspire to acquire the desires we admire. Inspiration is the key into motivation and revelation. Unless we remain inspired, we end up in mockery and misery in life.

"But there is a spirit in man: and the inspiration of the Almighty giveth them understanding."
Job 32:8

----Examples of those who overcame life challenges

Helen Keller: *Lost her sight and hearing due to a mysterious fever when she was only 18 months old. She overcame her deafness and blindness to become a strong, educated woman who spoke about, and promoted, women's rights.*

Winston Churchill: *Overcame a stuttering problem and poor performance in school to become Prime Minister of the United Kingdom he remains one of the most influential political leaders of the twentieth century. He was also known for his powerful and rousing speeches.*

Determination, resilience, and persistence enabled all of these great people to push past their adversities and prevail. If they could do it, surely the rest of us can summon the strength and courage to do overcome our adversities also.

CONSIDER THE FOLLOWING:

1) STRENGTH

2) WEAKNESS

3) THREATS

4) OPPORTUNITY

STRENGTH:

"A man's gift maketh room for him, and bringeth him before great men."
Proverb 18:16

It is scripturally correct to take advantage of our rea of strength in life. God gave us special gift called (talent) to bring out the best in us and the best in others around us. We must therefore utilize whatever gift God has given us to effect and impact the world around us.

WEAKNESS:

"You will remain a total failure until you discover your weakness in life"-Franklin N Abazie

Apostle Paul said *"And lest I should be exalted above measure through the abundance of the revelations, there was given to me a thorn in the flesh, the messenger of Satan to buffet me, lest I should be exalted above measure. For this thing I besought the Lord thrice, that it might depart from me. And he said unto me, My grace is sufficient for thee: for my strength is made perfect in weakness. Most gladly therefore will I rather glory in my infirmities that the power of Christ may rest upon me."* (2 Cor 12:7-9)

I believe by now we all have known our area of weakness in life. Some people cannot handle money. They lack the discipline to handle money. People will never trust you with money because you are weak in handling money. We must discover our weakness in life and deal with that sin that easily beset us in the name of Jesus.

THREATS:

Unless we come to term that everybody is not our friend, we remain vulnerable to the assault of the devil. In this race of life there are people to avoid. *"...and avoid them"* (Romans 16:17) There also people to *"turn away"* (2 Timothy 3:5) We must recognize our threat and take desperate measures against coming into contact with them. Joseph ran away from the threat of King Herod...

"But when Herod was dead, behold, an angel of the Lord appeareth in a dream to Joseph in Egypt, Saying, Arise, and take the young child and his mother, and go into the land of Israel: for they are dead which sought the young child's life. And he arose, and took the young child and his mother, and came into the land of Israel. But when he heard that Archelaus did reign in Judaea in the room of his father Herod, he was afraid to go thither: notwithstanding, being warned of God in a dream, he turned aside into the parts of Galilee. - Mathew 2:19-22

Moses ran away from threat of his life in Egypt.

"And the Lord said unto Moses in Midian, Go, return into Egypt: for all the men are dead which sought thy life. And Moses took his wife and his sons, and set them upon an ass, and he returned to the land of Egypt: and Moses took the rod of God in his hand."
Exodus 4:19-20

Godly wisdom demand we stay away from our threat in life.

OPPORTUNITY:

In times of adversity lies plenty of opportunities for us in life. As long as we are humbled, meek, and sincere, we will always see opportunities in times of famine and hardship. But some arrogant proud people will never see opportunities in the midst of great impossibilities.

ACCESS INTO THE SUPERNATURAL

BE BORN AGAIN:

We must be born again for us to experience the supernatural and mentorship.

Jesus answered and said unto him, Verily, verily, I say unto thee, Except a man be born again, he cannot see the kingdom of God. Nicodemus saith unto him, How can a man be born when he is old? can he enter the second time into his mother's womb, and be born? Jesus answered, Verily, verily, I say unto thee, Except a man be born of water and of the Spirit, he cannot enter into the kingdom of God.

That which is born of the flesh is flesh; and

that which is born of the Spirit is spirit. Marvel not that I said unto thee, Ye must be born again. The wind bloweth where it listeth, and thou hearest the sound thereof, but canst not tell whence it cometh, and whither it goeth: so is every one that is born of the Spirit.

We must therefore obey the voice of the Lord, confess him as Lord and savior then we can learn from his teaching and position our lives to encounter the supernatural. (John 3:3-8)

THE FEAR OF GOD:

One of the greatest channels to position our lives to encounter the supernatural is to covet the spirit of the fear of God. The fear of the Lord is the beginning of wisdom: and the knowledge of the holy is understanding.
Proverb 9:10

RIGHTEOUS LIFESTYLE:

It may take a longer time, but over the cause of your life time it will show. Righteousness is a virtue that tell everybody around you, the way you live, the way you do business and the way you operate. "For the vision is yet for an appointed time, but at the end it shall speak, and not lie: though it tarry, wait for it; because it will surely come, it will not tarry." (Hab 2:3)

INTEGRITY:

The integrity of the upright shall guide them:......
Proverb 11:3

As long as you carry integrity in your heart, it will guide your life from all assaults and attacks of the devil. So he fed them according to the integrity of his heart; and guided them by the skillfulness of his hands. (Psalm 78:72)

AGREEMENT:

Until you agree with the Holy Spirit by believe God's word to be true, you will forever suffer frustration. Once you agree with the Holy Spirit, you are guaranteed access into the supernatural. Again I say unto you, That if two of you shall agree on earth as touching any thing that they shall ask, it shall be done for them of my Father which is in heaven. (Mathew 18:19)

For where two or three are gathered together in my name, there am I in the midst of them. (Mathew 18:20) **Remember** …. The Lord thy God in the midst of thee is mighty. (Zeph 3:17)

SOUL WINNING:

It is written... *"and he that winneth souls is wise."* (Proverb 11:30) Soul winning is the gate way into the supernatural. As long as you win souls for Jesus he will decorate your life and destiny.

REASONS WHY WE MUST WORSHIP GOD

--HE IS OUR CREATOR--

1) We must worship Him, because He is our creator.

2) We must worship Him, because He is sovereign.

3) We must worship Him, because we are made in His image.

4) We must worship Him, because our worship attracts His presence.

5) We must worship Him, for our faith in Him to grow.

6) We must worship Him, to nourish and reactivate our spirit man.

7) We must worship Him, because it activates our faith in Him.

8) We must worship Him, to retain the Joy of the Lord.

9) We worship Him to evict depression, envy, and malice.

10) We worship Him to be happy and to escape strive and hatred.

11) We worship Him to escape bitterness, stress, anger, and misery.

BENEFITS OF OUR WORSHIP

1) Worship is medicinal, it heals our soul, body and spirit man.

2) Worship is supernatural, it position us for constant victory in life.

3) Worship is spiritual, it grants us hope and faith in Him.

4) Worship is a mystery, it keeps us on the winning side of life.

5) Worship is faithful, it gives us encourages us to put us the fight.

6) Worship is strengthening, it reduces the size of our problem.

7) Worship is devotional, it proves our loyalty.

8) Worship is humbling, it proves our meekness before God.

9) Worship is power, it grants us access into signs and wonders.

10) Worship is divine, it accelerates divine intervention.

11) Worship is pleasing, God takes pleasure in it.

12) Worship is a treasure, it catches the attention of God.

13) Worship is rewarding, it brings God into our trials.

14) Worship is reciprocal, it provokes God to act

15) Worship is glorifying, it magnifies God in our situation.

16) Worship is a blessing, it opens the flood gate of heaven.

17) Worship is our responsibility, it delivers us out of obscurity.

18) Worship is deliverance, it releases us out of captivity.

19) Worship is deeper, God looks for us to prove His divinity.

20) Worship is a reminder, God remembers His promises.

21) Worship is protection, we secure His protection.

22) Worship is unity, it grants us angelic help.

WHAT TO DO WHEN MIRACLE SEEMS TO BE DELAYED:

1. Praise God even in times of trouble, trial, and tribulations.

2. Be expectant- expect God to move beyond imagination.

3) Be willing and Obedient-God look at your obedient in times of delay.

4) Be focus—God expect us to pay relevant attention to details.

5) Do not quit- If we must emerge winners, quitting is not an option.

6) Be positive—it can only get better so be positive.

7) Be optimistic--- Your case is different so be optimistic in life.

8) Develop all possibility mentality—every limitation is within you faith.

WHAT TO DO WHEN OTHERS SEEM TO GET THEIR MIRACLES:

----Hope in God----

If God has done something to other individuals, we must celebrate with them. It is a sign that we are next in line. Whenever we celebrate with others, we are next in line for a miracle. We must hope and have faith in God.

"I have rejoiced in the way of thy testimonies, as much as in all riches."
Psalms 119:14

God does not look like man look, because God searches the heart, we must therefore be glad to hear the testimonies of others. It is written, *"Thy testimonies also are my delight and my counselors."* (Psalm 119:124)

----Have faith in God----

Unless we develop strong faith and confidence in God we will never experience our miracles. Often God will put us on a test, unless we pass the faith test we will never encounter God. *"…. God left him, to try him, that he might know all that was in his heart."* (2 Chr 32:31)

----*We must be focused*----

It is written *"For his anger endureth but a moment; in his favour is life: weeping may endure for a night, but joy cometh in the morning."* (Psalm 30:5) *"One man said unless we focus we will end up like locust, and unless we fast we will not last."* Every time we are distracted we miss our miracle from God. Focus comes with dedication and discipline in life. Jesus promised us that as long as we remain faithful and focused, we will never encounter the supernatural.

"And Jesus said unto him, No man, having put his hand to the plough, and looking back, is fit for the kingdom of God."
Luke 9:62

----WHAT TO DO WHEN THINGS GET WORSE WHILE SEEKING GOD----

----Trust in God----

It is written *"Trust in the Lord with all thine heart; and lean not unto thine own understanding. In all thy ways acknowledge him, and he shall direct thy paths."* (Proverb 3:5-6) In the midst of calamity and prevailing circumstances we must trust in God.

"Although the fig tree shall not blossom, neither shall fruit be in the vines; the labour of the olive shall fail, and the fields shall yield no meat; the flock shall be cut off from the fold, and there shall be no herd in the stalls: Yet I will rejoice in the Lord, I will joy in the God of my salvation."
Habakkuk 3:17-18

----Do not be anxious - Our change will come at His will----

----When the battle gets worse, the miracle gets better and bigger----

----Whenever we are seeking God, every negative change of situation is a setup for our promotion----

----Those who seek God are never stranded - There is always a miracle for them----

BREAKTHROUGH PRAYER POINTS

"And this is the confidence that we have in him, that, if we ask any thing according to his will, he heareth us."
1 John 5:14

Holy Spirit of God frustrate and disappoint, every one that is against my life and family, in the name of Jesus.

Father Lord destroy every demonic networks and traps against my progress in life in the name of Jesus.

Fire of God, destroy every demonic projection and curses against my life and destiny in the name of Jesus.

Every spell and curses pronounced against my destiny, break, in the name of Jesus.

Hand of God cage every power militating against my rising in life, in the name of Jesus.

Power of God silent every voice raising a counter motion against my elevation, in the mighty name of Jesus.

Blood of Jesus neutralize every spirit of Balaam hired to hinder my life, ministry, and career, the name of Jesus.

Fire of God destroy every curse that I have brought into my life through ignorance and disobedience, break by fire, in the name of Jesus.

Ancient of day destroy every power harassing my ministry in the name of Jesus.

Father God deliver me from invincible forces militating against my life and destiny.

Power of God frustrate every coven and demonic network, designed to frustrate and hinder my success in life, in the name of Jesus.

I dismantle every strong hold designed to imprison my talent in the mighty name of Jesus.

I reject every cycle of frustration, in the name of Jesus.
Power of God paralyze every agent assigned to frustrate my life in the name of Jesus.

Finger of God, grant me supernatural speed against all my contenders in the name of Jesus.

By the blood of Jesus, I destroy every familiar spirit caging my life and career.

Fire of God arrest every demonic agents, assigned to police my destiny and marriage.

By the blood of Jesus, I proclaim no weapon fashioned against me shall ever prosper.

Holy Spirit of God break me through and forward in life in the mighty name of Jesus.

God, smash me and renew my strength, in the name of Jesus.
Holy Spirit, open my eyes to see beyond the visible to the invisible, in the name of Jesus.

Father Lord grant me strength and power in the name of Jesus
O Lord, liberate my spirit to follow the leading of the Holy Spirit.

Holy Spirit, teach me to pray through problems instead of praying about, it in the name of Jesus.

Father Lord, deliver me from the false accusation in life, in the name of Jesus

By the blood of Jesus, every evil spiritual padlock and evil chain hindering my success, be roasted, in the name of Jesus.

By the blood of Jesus I rebuke every spirit of spiritual deafness and blindness in my life, in the name of Jesus.

Father Lord, empower me to dominate the enemy of my destiny in the name of Jesus.

Jesus Christ of Nazareth, heal my infirmities in the name of Jesus

Lord, anoint my eyes and my ears that they may see and hear wondrous things from heaven.

Father Lord, anoint me with power and authority to dominate all my enemies in the name of Jesus.

Fire of God roast every giant rising up against my life and career.

Holy Spirit of God destroy all my oppressors in the name of Jesus.

Angels of good new, bring my good news to me in the mighty name of Jesus.

Every strong man holding me down, lose your hold now in the name of Jesus.

I nullify every demonic prediction over my life in the name of Jesus.

By the blood of Jesus, I flush out every polluted deposit of the enemy in my life.

By the blood of Jesus, I paralyze every enemy of my promotion in the name of Jesus.

Father Lord, destroy any power tormenting my life that is not from you.

Holy Ghost fire, ignite the fire of revival in my life.

By the blood of Jesus, I declare victory over every conflicting trial

By the Blood of Jesus, I command the arrest of every demonic spirit, militating against my life.

By the blood of Jesus, I proclaimed the blood of Jesus, over every device of the enemy.

By the blood of Jesus, I revoke stagnation and hardship over my life in the name of Jesus.

Holy Ghost fire, destroy every satanic arrangement in my life, in the name of Jesus.

CONCLUSION

"Winners never quit in life"

This book is designed to remind us of our winning root in Christ Jesus Christ. Unless we are a winner in life, we are merely faking our Christianity. Jesus is a winner. The bible says *"Now we, brethren, as Isaac was, are the children of promise."* (Gal 4:28).

but recall with me...

"And if ye be Christ's, then are ye Abraham's seed, and heirs according to the promise."
Gal 3:29

Our root is in Christ. I therefore command and admonish you in the way of the Lord to wake up from every trial and obstacle and embrace your victory. We must begin to live a winning lifestyle of victory the remaining days of our lives.

In my opinion obstacles are design to test our faith and for our triumphant living and dominion. We must prove the hand of God upon our lives by proving the devil defeating the devil and proving all evil counsel and appearance wrong.

ARE YOU WINNING IN YOUR AREA OF CALLING IN LIFE?

"Wherefore the rather, brethren, give diligence to make your calling and election sure: for if ye do these things, ye shall never fall."
2 Peter 1:9

"Who hath saved us, and called us with an holy calling, not according to our works, but according to his own purpose and grace, which was given us in Christ Jesus before the world began."
2 Timothy 1:10

Unless you are in command of you calling in life, you will forever live in frustration and want of all things in life.

"For I would that all men were even as I myself. But every man hath his proper gift of God, one after this manner, and another after that."
1 Cor 7:7

"But as God hath distributed to every man, as the Lord hath called every one, so let him walk. And so ordain I in all churches."
1 Cor 7:17

"Let every man abide in the same calling wherein he was called."
1 Cor 7:20

"Brethren, let every man, wherein he is called, therein abide with God."
1 Cor 7:24

Perhaps only this page out of this entire book will make a positive impact upon your life. Permit me to ask you this question here today, *Are you winning and succeeding in the area God had called in life?* If the answer is yes, then keep doing what you are doing right to generate result but if no let me help you here immediately.

FAVOR CONFESSION

Father thank you for making me righteous and accepted through the blood of Jesus Christ. Because of that, I am blessed and highly favored by God. I am the subject of your affection. Your favor surrounds me as a shield, and the first thing that people see around me is your favored shield.

Thank you that I have favor with you and man today. All day long people go out of their way to bless me and help me. I have favor with everyone that I deal with today. Doors that were once closed are now opened for me. I receive preferential treatment, and I have special privileges, I am Gods favored child.

No good thing will he withhold from me. Because of Gods favor my enemies cannot triumph over my life. I have supernatural increase and promotion. I declare restoration to everything that the devil has stolen from my life. I have honor in the midst of my adversaries and an increase in assets, especially in real estate and expansion of territories.

Because I am highly favored by God, I experience great victories, supernatural turnarounds, and miraculous breakthrough in the midst of great impossibilities. I receive recognition, prominence, and honor. Petitions are granted to me even by ungodly authorities. Policies, rules, regulations, and laws are changed and reverse on my behalf.

I win battles that I don't even have to fight, because God fights them for me. This is the day, the set time and the designated moment for me to experience the free favor of God, that profusely and lavishly abound on my behalf in Jesus name. Amen.

YOU MUST BE BORN AGAIN

If you are a born again Christian; we like to encourage you in your Christian life. If you are not a born again Christian we can help you here receive genuine salvation. (2 Cor 5:17) Therefore if any man be in Christ, he is a new creature: old things are passed away; behold, all things are become new.

Now repeat this Prayer after me

Say Lord Jesus, I accept you today, as my Lord and my savior, forgive me of my sins wash me with your blood. Right now, I believe, I am sanctified, I am save, I am free, I am free from the Power of sin to serve the Lord Jesus. Thank you Lord for saving me. Amen.

Congratulation: YOU ARE NOW...

...A BORN AGAIN CHRISTIAN.

AGAIN I SAY TO YOU - CONGRATULATIONS!

What must I do to determine my divine visitation?

To determine divine visitation you must be born again! The word says as many as received him, to them gave He power to become the sons of God. Even to them that believe on his name.

To qualify for divine visitation do the following sincerely

1) Acknowledge that you are a sinner and that He died for you. (Romans 3:23)

2) Repent of your sins. (Acts 3:19, Luke 13:5, 2 Peter 3:9)

3) Believe in your heart that Jesus died for your sin.(Romans 10:10)

4) Confess Jesus as the Lord over your life. (Romans 10:10, Acts 2:21)

Now repeat this Prayer after me

Say Lord Jesus, I accept you today, as my Lord and my savior, forgive me of my sins wash me with your blood. Right now, I believe, I am sanctified, I am save, I am free, I am free from the Power of sin to serve the Lord Jesus. Thank you Lord for saving me. Amen.

Congratulations: YOU ARE NOW...

...A BORN AGAIN CHRISTIAN.

AGAIN I SAY TO YOU - CONGRATULATIONS!

I adjure you to watch the Spirit of God bear witness with your Spirit confirming His word with signs following. The word says The Spirit itself beareth witness with our spirit, that we are the children of God. Join a bible believing church or join us on our weekly and Sunday worship services at 343 Sanford Avenue Newark New Jersey 07106.

WISDOM KEYS

1) Every Productive Society is a society heading to the top

2) Millions of Nigerians run away from Nigeria, very few Nigerians stay in Nigeria.

3) My decision to return Nigeria is the will of God for my life

4) My short coming in America after 18 years, trained me to be wise, to think, reflect and reason appropriately.

5) If you train your mind to reason it will train your hands to earn money.

6) It is absurd to use the money of the heathen to build the kingdom of the living God.

7) Every Ministry reveals its agenda and goal either at the beginning or at the end. Be careful of your life it is your first Ministry.

8) The average American mind is conditioned for a continual quest to get new things and (discard the former) and throw away old things.

9) When I considered well, my BMW jeep became my initial deposit for the work of the ministry in Nigeria

10) Money will never fall from any Treebank, Treasury Department or person. Make up your mind to be independent today.

11) Everyone is waiting for you to change your mind until you change your thinking nothing changes around you.

12) Multiple academic degrees in other discipline gave me the chance to think, reflect and reason

13) What so everyone are thinking and reflecting at the moment reveals you to the time and the now factor

14) All events and intents are the product of precise thought processes, accurate reason every event is designed for a designated timeline

15) Wisdom is your ability to think, to create and invent. If you can think wise enough you will come out of penury

16) The distance between you and success is your creative ability to think reason and reflect accurate.

17) Success is the result of hard work, commitment resolve and determination learning from past mistakes and failing.

18) If you organize your mind you have organized your life and destiny.

19) There is a thin line between success and failure. If you look above and beyond you are on your way to success.

20) Wealth is your ability to think, power is your ability to reason and success is your ability to be informed.

21) If you can make use of your mind by thinking and reasoning God will make use of your life and destiny.

22) Think and Be Great

23) Reflect, Reason, think and be great

24) Famous people are born of woman

25) That you will make it is your intention; that you will survive is your resolve, that you will succeed with changes is your determination, personal efforts and hard work.

26) No man was born a failure. Lack of vision is the end product of failure.

27) Working with mental patients encourages and aspire me to be a productive observant and dedicated to my assignment.

28) Successful people are not magicians, it is the will power combined with hard work, and determination and a resolve to succeed that make them succeed.

29) In the unequivocal state of the mind, intention is not a location or a position it is the state of the mind.

30) So many people think that they think. The mind is used to think reflect and reason. You will remain blind with your eye open until you can see with your mind by thinking.

31) There is no favoritism in accurate and precise calculation

32) Although knowledge is power, information is the key and gateway to a great future.

33) It will take the hand of God to move the hand of man.

34) With the backing of the great wise God, nothing will disconnect you from your inheritance.

35) As long as you have wisdom and understanding of God, Satan and evil cannot manipulate your life and destiny.

36) You have come this far by yourself judgment and decision you have made in the past, now lean and listen to God for another dimension of greatness.

37) Great people are common people it is extra ordinary effort and the price of sacrifice that produces greatness.

38) As a mental direct care worker I saw a great pastor and a motivational speaker within myself.

39) Menial job does not reduce your self-worth, until you resolve to achieve greatness see greatness in all you do; you will never count in your community.

40) The principle of Jesus will solve your gambling and addiction problems

41) The man of Jesus will lead you into heaven,

42) Everyone have their self-appraisal and what they think about you. Until you discover yourself other opinion about you will alter the real you.

43) Supervisors and directors are just a position in the chain of command in a work place. Never allow your supervisor hierarchy to alter your opinion about yourself.

44) Everyone can come out of debt if they make up their mind.

45) That I am not a decision maker at work does not diminish my contribution to my world.

46) Although it appears like it was a poor decision to accept a direct care employment at a psychiatric hospital as I reflect of my nine

years of experience, it became apparent that I have learnt and experienced enough for my next assignment.

47) Self-encouragement and determination is a resolve of the heart.

48) If you are determined to make a difference, and do the things that make a difference you will eventually make a difference.

49) Good things do not come easy

50) Short cuts will cut your life short.

51) Those who look ahead move ahead.

52) Life is all about making an impact. In your life time strive to make an impact in your community.

53) Make friends and connect with people who are moving ahead of you in life.

54) If you can look around well you have come a long way in your life, made a lot of difference and realized a lot of success in life.

55) If you are my old friend, hurry up to reach out to me before I become a stranger to you.

56) Everything I am blessed with inspirations from God, that change my definition and interpretation of the world around me.

57) I thought I was stagnant and lonely until I looked around and noticed my children running around and my wife cooking.

58) At 40 I resigned my Job to seek the Lord forever.

59) My ministry took a drastic rise to the top when the wisdom of God visited me with knowledge and understanding.

60) You will be a better person if you understand the characteristics of your personality – your mood swings attitudes and habits.

61) It is the seed of love you sow into the heart of a child and a woman that you reap in due time.

62) Love is not selfish, love share everything including the concealed secrets of the mind.

63) As long as you have a prayer life and a bible; you will never feel lonely, rejected and idle in the race of life.

64) When good friends disconnect from you, let them go, they might have seen something new in a different direction.

65) Confidence in yourself and in God is the only way to bring you out of captivity

66) Never train a child to waste his/her time.

67) The mind is the greatest assets of a great future.

68) You walk by common sense run by principles and fly by instruction.

69) Those who fly in flight of life fly alone.

70) Up in the air you are alone. No one can toll you accept the compass of knowledge and information

71) I have seen a tolling vehicle I have seen a tolling ship I have never seen a tolling airplane.

72) I exercise my judgment and make a decision every minute of the day.

73) Decisions are crucial, critical and vital with reference to your future.

74) So many people wish for a great future. You can only work towards a great future.

75) Your celebrity status began when you discovered your talent. What are you good at? Work at it with all commitment.

76) Prayers will sustain you but the wisdom of God will prosper you.

77) When I met Oyedepo, his teachings changed my perspective, but when I met Ibiyeomie; His teaching changed my perception.

78) I will be successful in ministry if only I concentrate and focus my energy in the work of the ministry.

79) It took the late Dr. Vincent Pearle Norman's book to open my mind towards kingdom success.

CHAPTER 3
PRAYER OF SALVATION

It will profit us nothing as a ministry if after reading this book, your salvation is still questionable. I long to see you saved and delivered from all the wiles and schemes of the devil.

ARE YOU SAVED?

The honest truth is that the Lord Jesus really does not know you unless you are saved. For as many as are led by the Spirit of God, they are the sons of God. *"For ye have not received the spirit of bondage again to fear; but ye have received the Spirit of adoption, whereby we cry, Abba, Father. The Spirit itself beareth witness with our spirit, that we are the children of God."* (Romans 8:14-16)

What must I do to determine my divine visitation?

To determine divine visitation you must be born again! The word says as many as received him, to them gave He power to become the sons of God. Even to them that believe on his name.

To qualify for divine visitation do the following sincerely

1) Acknowledge that you are a sinner and that He died for you. (Romans 3:23)

2) Repent of your sins. (Acts 3:19, Luke 13:5, 2 Peter 3:9)

3) Believe in your heart that Jesus died for your sin.(Romans 10:10)

4) Confess Jesus as the Lord over your life. (Romans 10:10, Acts 2:21)

Now repeat this Prayer after me

Say Lord Jesus, I accept you today, as my Lord and my savior, forgive me of my sins wash me with your blood. Right now, I believe, I am sanctified, I am save, I am free, I am free from the Power of sin to serve the Lord Jesus. Thank you Lord for saving me. Amen.

Congratulations: YOU ARE NOW...

...A BORN AGAIN CHRISTIAN.

AGAIN I SAY TO YOU - CONGRATULATIONS!

I adjure you to watch the Spirit of God bear witness with your Spirit confirming His word with signs following. The word says The Spirit itself beareth witness with our spirit, that we are the children of God.

MIRACLE CARE OUTREACH

"...But that the members should have the same care one for another"
1 Cor 12:25

We are all members of the body of Christ. Jesus commanded us to love our neighbor as ourselves. This includes caring for one another as a member of one body. True love is expressed in caring and giving. The word says for God so Love He gave….

Reach out to someone in need of Jesus, help someone in crisis find Christ. Look out and prove your love to Jesus by caring and inviting your friends and associates to find Jesus the Healer.

Invite your friends to our Home Care Cell Fellowship (Miracle chapel Intl Satellite fellowship) In the USA at 33 Schley Street Newark New Jersey 07112.

If you are in Nigeria—MIRACLE OF GOD MINISTRIES, A.K.A "MIRACLE CHAPEL INTL" Mpama –Egbu-Owerri Imo state Nigeria.

(Home Care Cell fellowship Group). We meet every Tuesday at 6:00pm-7:00pm.

LIFE IS NOT ALL ABOUT DURATION BUT ITS ALL ABOUT DONATION

What does the above statement mean?....

Life consists not in accumulation of material wealth.(Luke12:15) But it's all about liberality.... meaning- what you can give and share with others. (Proverb 11:25) When you live for others--You live forever- because you out live your generation by the legacy you live behind after you depart into glory to be with the Lord. But when you live to yourself - you are reduced to self—you are easily forgotten when you die and depart in glory.

Permit me to admonish you today to live your life to be a blessing to a soul connected to you today. I want you to know that so many souls are connected and looking up to you, and through you so many souls will be saved and rescued from destruction. Will you disciple someone today to find Jesus Christ?

As a genuine Christian; it is your duty to evangelize Jesus Christ to all you meet on your way. Jesus is still in the healing business-Jesus is still doing miracles from time of old to now. Therefore tell someone about Jesus Christ today, disciple and bring them to Church. *Philip findeth Nathanael...* (John 1:45)

Please to prove the sincerity of your love

for God today; please become a soul winner. The dignity of your Christianity is hidden in your boldness to proclaim and evangelize Jesus Christ to all you meet on your way. There is a question mark on the integrity of your Christianity until you become a life soul winner. Invite someone to join us worship the Lord Jesus this coming Sunday. Amen.

MIRACLE OF GOD MINISTRIES

PILLARS OF THE COMMISSION

We Believe Preach and Practice the following

1) We believe and preach Salvation to every living human being

2) We believe and preach Repentance and forgiveness of sins

3) We believe and preach the baptism of the Holy Spirit and Spiritual gifts

4) We believe and teach the Prosperity

5) We believe and preach Divine Healing and Miracles (Signs & Wonder)

6) We believe and preach Faith

7) We believe and Proclaim the Power of God (Supernatural)

8) We believe and Proclaim Praise & Worship to God

9) We believe and preach Wisdom

10) We believe and preach Holiness (Consecration)

11) We believe and preach Vision

12) We believe and teach the Word of God

13) We believe and teach Success

14) We believe and practice Prayer

15) We believe and teach Deliverance

This 15 stones form the Pillars of Our Commission. Become part of this church family and follow this great move of God.

Chapter 3   Prayer of Salvation

--MY HEART FELT PRAYER FOR YOU--

It is always my joy and pleasure to see you saved. It is always my joy to know that you will make heaven with us. But I rejoice more with you, when I hear your testimonies and encounters with God. One of the reason why I write is to spread the gospel of Jesus Christ in print. I therefore encourage you to get in touch with any of our materials. We offer so many materials available for you, from books, magazine, mp3 tapes, sermon outlines, and brochure. I guarantee you, it will highly help your faith and your walk with our Lord Jesus Christ.

Now let me Pray for you:

Father God I thank you because all things work together for our good. Lord even today demonstrate you awesome power that is unique and unlimited in dimension unto this precious loved one reading this book now. Lord God increase their faith by granting them unprecedented testimonies. Lord do that no man can do and take all the glory.
In Jesus Mighty name. Amen

ETERNITY IS REAL!

It will profit us nothing as a ministry if you finish reading this book without making plans for heaven. You must make conscious plans to make heaven because eternity is real.

Indeed we live in an immoral time, sin has gained grounds and promotion that even the righteous are tempted to fall short of the glory of God.

You might ask me, what must I do to be saved?

As long as we believe and repent God is willing to forgive and to restore our lives

"And they said, Believe on the Lord Jesus Christ, and thou shalt be saved, and thy house."
Acts 16:31

"Salvation is possible only through the name of our Lord Jesus Christ. Neither is there salvation in any other: for there is none other name under heaven given among men, whereby we must be saved." (Acts 4:12)

I admonish you therefore to think twice before you commit those sins that not only easily beset you but also separates you far away from God. As long as you repent even now, God is more than willing to restore and save your life from eternal hell fire. And make straight paths for your feet, lest that which is lame be turned out of the way; but let it rather be healed. Follow peace with all men, and holiness, without which no man shall see the Lord. (Hebrew 12:13-14)

Make conscious plans to make heaven. Change the way you approach things and God will restore and forgive you of all your sins. Amen

ABOUT THE AUTHOR

Rev Franklin N Abazie is the founding and Presiding Pastor of Miracle of God Ministries with headquarters in Newark, New Jersey USA and a branch church in Owerri- Imo State Nigeria. He is following the footsteps of one of his mentors, Oral Roberts (Healing Evangelist) of the blessed memory. The Lord passed Oral Roberts healing mantle two days before he went to be with the Lord at age 91 into the hand of healing evangelist-Rev Franklin N Abazie in a vision.

In all his services the Power and Presence of God is present to heal all in his audience. He is an ordained man of God with a Healing Ministry reviving the healing and miracle ministry of Jesus Christ of Nazareth.

Pastor Franklin N Abazie, is called by God with a unique mandate: **"THE MOMENT IS DUE TO IMPACT YOUR WORLD THROUGH THE REVIVAL OF THE HEALING & MIRACLE MINISTRY OF JESUS CHRIST OF NAZARETH**

I AM SENDING YOU TO RESTORE HEALTH UNTO THEE AND I WILL HEAL THEE OF THY WOUNDS. SAID THE LORD OF HOST"

He is a gifted ardent Teacher of the word of God who operates also in the office of a Prophet, generating and attracting undeniable signs & wonders, special miracles and healings, with apostolic fireworks of the Holy Ghost. He is the founding and presiding senior Pastor of this fast growing Healing ministry. He has written over 86 inspirational, healing and transforming books covering almost all aspect of divine healing and life. He is happily married and blessed with children.

BOOKS BY REV FRANKLIN N ABAZIE

1) *The Outcome of Faith*
2) *Understanding the secret of prevailing Prayers*
3) *Commanding Abundance*
4) *Understanding the secret of the man God uses*
5) *Activating my due Season*
6) *Overcoming Divine Verdicts*
7) *The Outcome of Divine Wisdom*
8) *Understanding God's Restoration Mandate*
9) *Walking in the Victory and Authority of the truth*
10) *Gods Covenant Exemption*
11) *Destiny Restoration Pillars*
12) *Provoking Acceptable Praise*
13) *Understanding Divine Judgment*
14) *Activating Angelic Re-enforcement*
15) *Provoking Un-Merited Favor*
16) *The Benefits of the Speaking faith*
17) *Understanding Divine Arrangement*
18) *How to Keep Your Healing*
19) *Understanding the mysteries of the Speaking Faith*
20) *Understanding the mysteries of Prophetic healing*
21) *Operating under the Rules of Creative Healing*
22) *Understanding the joy of Breakthrough*
23) *Understanding the Mystery of Breakthrough*
24) *Understanding Divine Prosperity*
25) *Understanding Divine Healing*
26) *Retaining Your Inheritance*
27) *Overcoming confusing Spirit*
28) *Commanding Angelic Escorts*
29) *Enforcing Your inheritance in Christ Jesus*

30) Understanding Your Guardian Angels
31) Overcoming the Dominion of Sin
32) Understanding the Voice of God
33) The Outstanding benefits of the Anointing
34) The Audacity of the Blood of Jesus
35) Walking in the Reality of the Anointing
36) Escaping the Nightmare of Poverty
37) Understanding Your Harvest Season
38) Activating Your Success Buttons
39) Overcoming the forces of Darkness
40) Overcoming the devices of the devil
41) Overcoming Demonic agents
42) Overcoming the sorrows of failure
43) Rejecting the Sorrows of failure
44) Resisting the Sorrows of Poverty
45) The Restoring broken Marriages.
46) Redeeming Your Days
47) The force of Vision
48) Overcoming the forces of ignorance
49) Understanding the sacrifice of small beginning
50) The might of small beginning
51) Understanding the mysteries of Prophesy
52) Overcoming Dream nightmares
53) Breaking the shackles of the curse of the law
54) Understanding the Joy of harvest
55) Wisdom for Signs & Wonders
56) Wisdom for generational Impact
57) Wisdom for Marriage Stability
58) Understanding the number of your Days
59) Enforcing Your Kingdom Rights
60) Escaping the traps of immoralities
61) Escaping the trap of Poverty
62) Accessing Biblical Prosperity

63) Accessing True Riches in Christ
64) Silencing the Voice of the Accuser
65) Overcoming the forces of oppositions
66) Quenching the voice of the avenger
67) Silencing demonic Prediction & Projection
68) Silencing Your Mocker
69) Understanding the Power of the Holy Ghost
70) Understanding the baptism of Power
71) The Mystery of the Blood of Jesus
72) Understanding the Mystery of Sanctification
73) Understanding the Power of Holiness
74) Understanding the forces of Purity & Righteousness
75) Activating the Forces of Vengeance
76) Appreciating the Mystery of Restoration
77) Overcoming the Projection & Prediction of the enemy
78) Engaging the mystery of the blood
79) Commanding the Power of the Speaking faith
80) Uprooting the forces against Your Rising
81) Overcoming mere success syndrome
82) Understanding Divine Sentence
83) Understanding the Mystery of Praise
84) Understanding the Author of Faith
85) The Mystery of the finisher of faith
86) Attracting Supernatural Favor

MIRACLE OF GOD MINISTRIES

*NIGERIA CRUSADE
2012*

MIRACLE OF GOD MINISTRIES

NIGERIA CRUSADE 2012

MIRACLE OF GOD MINISTRIES

NIGERIA CRUSADE
2012

www.ingramcontent.com/pod-product-compliance
Lightning Source LLC
Chambersburg PA
CBHW071745080526
44588CB00013B/2155